ISBN: 9781290398633

Published by:
HardPress Publishing
8345 NW 66TH ST #2561
MIAMI FL 33166-2626

Email: info@hardpress.net
Web: http://www.hardpress.net

THE

RAPE OF THE LOCK

BY

ALEXANDER POPE

INSEL-VERLAG/LEIPZIG

THE RAPE OF THE LOCK

AN HEROI-COMICAL POEM

Written in the Year 1712

★

Nolueram, Belinda, tuos violare capillos;
Sed juvat, hoc precibus me tribuisse tuis.

MART.

TO MRS. ARABELLA FERMOR

MADAM,

I T WILL be in vain to deny that I have some regard for this piece, since I dedicate it to you; yet you may bear me witness, it was intended only to divert a few young ladies, who have good sense and good humour enough to laugh not only at their sex's little unguarded follies, but at their own. But as it was communicated with the aïr of a secret, it soon found its way into the world. An imperfect copy having been offered to a bookseller, you had the good-nature for my sake to consent to the publication of one more correct. This I was forced to, before I had executed half my design, for the machinery was entirely wanting to complete it.

The machinery, Madam, is a term invented by the critics, to signify that part which the deities, angels, or demons, are made to act in a poem; for the ancient poets are in one respect like many modern ladies: let an action be never so trivial in itself, they always make it appear of the utmost importance. These machines I determined to raise on a very new and odd foundation, the Rosicrucian doctrine of spirits.

I know how disagreeable it is to make use of hard words before a lady; but it is so much the concern of a poet to have his works understood, and particularly by your sex, that you must give me leave to explain two or three difficult terms.

The Rosicrucians are a people I must bring you acquainted with. The best account I know of them is in a French book called *Le Comte de Gabalis,* which, both in its title and size, is so like a novel, that many of the fair sex have read it for one by mistake. According to these gentlemen, the four elements are inhabited by spirits which they call Sylphs, Gnomes, Nymphs, and Salamanders. The Gnomes, or demons of earth, delight in mischief; but the Sylphs, whose habitation is in the air, are the best-conditioned creatures imaginable; for they say, any mortal may enjoy the most intimate familiarities with these gentle spirits, upon a condition very easy to all true adepts – an inviolate preservation of chastity.

As to the following cantos, all the passages of them are as fabulous as the vision at the beginning, or the transformation at the end (except the loss of your hair, which I always mention with reverence). The human persons are as fictitious as the airy ones; and the character of Belinda, as it is now managed, resembles you in nothing but in beauty.

If this poem had as many graces as there are in your person or in your mind, yet I could never hope it should pass through the world half so uncensured as you have done. But let its fortune be what it will, mine is happy enough to have given me this occasion of assuring you that I am, with the truest esteem,

    MADAM,
        Your most obedient, humble servant,

                            A. POPE.

CANTO I

WHAT dire offence from amorous causes springs,
What mighty contests rise from trivial things,
I sing; — this verse to Caryl, Muse! is due:
This e'en Belinda may vouchsafe to view:
Slight is the subject, but not so the praise,
If she inspire, and he approve my lays.

Say what strange motive, goddess! could compel
A well-bred lord to assault a gentle belle?
O say what stranger cause, yet unexplored,
Could make a gentle belle reject a lord?
In tasks so bold, can little men engage?
And in soft bosoms dwells such mighty rage?

Sol through white curtains shot a timorous ray,
And oped those eyes that must eclipse the day:
Now lap-dogs give themselves the rousing shake,

And sleepless lovers, just at twelve, awake:
Thrice rung the bell, the slipper knock'd the ground,
And the press'd watch return'd a silver sound.
Belinda still her downy pillow press'd,
Her guardian Sylph prolong'd the balmy rest:
'T was he had summon'd to her silent bed
The morning dream that hover'd o'er her head.
A youth more glittering than a birth-night beau
(That e'en in slumber caused her cheek to glow)
Seem'd to her ear his winning lips to lay,
And thus in whispers said, or seem'd to say:
  "Fairest of mortals, thou distinguish'd care
Of thousand bright inhabitants of air!
If e'er one vision touch'd thy infant thought,
Of all the nurse and all the priest have taught;
Of airy elves by moonlight shadows seen,
The silver token, and the circled green,
Or virgins visited by angel-powers,
With golden crowns and wreaths of heavenly flowers;
Hear, and believe! thy own importance know,

Nor bound thy narrow views to things below.

Some secret truths, from learned pride conceal'd.

To maids alone and children are reveal'd,

What, though no credit doubting wits may give,

The fair and innocent shall still believe.

Know then, unnumberd spirits round thee fly.

The light militia of the lower sky:

These, though unseen, are ever on the wing,

Hang o'er the box, and hover round the ring.

Think what an equipage thou hast in air,

And view with scorn two pages and a chair.

As now your own, our beings were of old,

And once enclosed in woman's beauteous mould;

Thence, by a soft transition we repair,

From earthly vehicles to those of air.

Think not, when woman's transient breath is fled,

That all her vanities at once are dead:

Succeeding vanities she still regards,

And though she plays no more, o'erlooks the cards.

Her joy in gilded chariots, when alive,

And love of ombre, after death survive.

For when the fair in all their pride expire,

To their first elements their souls retire:

The sprites of fiery termagants in flame

Mount up, and take a Salamander's name.

Soft yielding minds to water glide away,

And sip, with nymphs, their elemental tea.

The graver prude sinks downward to a Gnome,

In search of mischief still on earth to roam.

The light coquettes in Sylphs aloft repair,

And sport and flutter in the fields of air.

"Know farther yet; whoever fair and chaste

Rejects mankind, is by some Sylph embraced:

For, spirits, freed from mortal laws, with ease

Assume what sexes and what shapes they please.

What guards the purity of melting maids,

In courtly balls, and midnight masquerades,

Safe from the treacherous friend, the daring spark,

The glance by day, the whisper in the dark,

When kind occasion prompts their warm desires,

When music softens, and when dancing fires?
'T is but their Sylph, the wise celestials know,
Though honour is the word with men below.

   "Some nymphs there are, too conscious of their face,
For life predestined to the Gnomes' embrace.
These swell their prospects, and exalt their pride,
When offers are disdain'd, and love denied:
Then gay ideas crowd the vacant brain,
While peers, and dukes, and all their sweeping train,
And garters, stars, and coronets appear,
And in soft sounds, 'your grace' salutes their ear.
'T is these that early taint the female soul,
Instruct the eyes of young coquettes to roll,
Teach infant cheeks a hidden blush to know,
And little hearts to flutter at a beau.

   "Oft, when the world imagine women stray,
The Sylphs through mystic mazes guide their way,
Through all the giddy circle they pursue,
And old impertinence expel by new.
What tender maid but must a victim fall

To one man's treat, but for another's ball?

When Florio speaks, what virgin could withstand,

If gentle Damon did not squeeze her hand?

With varying vanities, from every part,

They shift the moving toy-shop of their heart;

Where wigs with wigs, with sword-knots sword-knots strive,

Beaux banish beaux, and coaches coaches drive.

This erring mortals levity may call;

Oh, blind to truth! the Sylphs contrive it all.

　　"Of these am I, who thy protection claim,

A watchful sprite, and Ariel is my name.　·

Late, as I ranged the crystal wilds of air,

In the clear mirror of thy ruling star

I saw, alas! some dread event impend,

Ere to the main this morning sun descend;

But Heaven reveals not what, or how, or where:

Warn'd by thy Sylph, oh pious maid, beware!

This to disclose is all thy guardian can:

Beware of all, but most beware of man!"

　　He said; when Shock, who thought she slept too long,

Leap'd up, and waked his mistress with his tongue.

'T was then, Belinda, if report say true,

Thy eyes first open'd on a billet-doux;

Wounds, charms, and ardours were no sooner read,

But all the vision vanish'd from thy head.

And now unveil'd, the toilet stands display'd,

Each silver vase in mystic order laid.

First robed in white, the nymph intent adores,

With head uncover'd, the cosmetic powers.

A heavenly image in the glass appears,

To that she bends, to that her eyes she rears;

The inferior priestess, at her altar's side,

Trembling, begins the sacred rites of pride.

Unnumber'd treasures ope at once, and here

The various offerings of the world appear;

From each she nicely culls with curious toil,

And decks the goddess with the glittering spoil.

This casket India's glowing gems unlocks,

And all Arabia breathes from yonder box.

The tortoise here and elephant unite,

Transform'd to combs, the speckled and the white.

Here files of pins extend their shining rows,

Puffs, powders, patches, Bibles, billet-doux.

Now awful Beauty puts on all its arms;

The fair each moment rises in her charms,

Repairs her smiles, awakens every grace,

And calls forth all the wonders of her face;

Sees by degrees a purer blush arise,

And keener lightnings quicken in her eyes.

The busy sylphs surround their darling care:

These set the head, and those divide the hair;

Some fold the sleeve, whilst others plait the gown;

And Betty's praised for labour not her own.

CANTO II

Not with more glories in the ethereal plain,

The sun first rises o'er the purpled main,

Than, issuing forth, the rival of his beams

Launch'd on the bosom of the silver'd Thames.

Fair nymphs and well-dress'd youths around her shone,

But every eye was fix'd on her alone.

On her white breast a sparkling cross she wore,

Which Jews might kiss, and infidels adore.

Her lively looks a sprightly mind disclose,

Quick as her eyes, and as unfix'd as those:

Favours to none, to all she smiles extends;

Oft she rejects, but never once offends.

Bright as the sun, her eyes the gazers strike,

And, like the sun, they shine on all alike.

Yet graceful ease, and sweetness void of pride,

Might hide her faults, if belles had faults to hide:
If to her share some female errors fall,
Look on her face, and you'll forget them all.

   This nymph, to the destruction of mankind,
Nourish'd two locks, which graceful hung behind
In equal curls, and well conspired to deck
With shining ringlets the smooth ivory neck.
Love in these labyrinths his slaves detains,
And mighty hearts are held in slender chains.
With hairy springes we the birds betray;
Slight lines of hair surprise the finny prey;
Fair tresses man's imperial race ensnare,
And beauty draws us with a single hair.

   The adventurous baron the bright locks admired;
He saw, he wish'd, and to the prize aspired.
Resolved to win, he meditates the way,
By force to ravish, or by fraud betray;
For when success a lover's toil attends,
Few ask if fraud or force attain'd his ends.

   For this, ere Phœbus rose, he had implored

Propitious Heaven, and every power adored;

But chiefly Love; to Love an altar built,

Of twelve vast French romances, neatly gilt.

There lay three garters, half a pair of gloves,

And all the trophies of his former loves.

With tender billet-doux he lights the pyre,

And breathes three amorous sighs to raise the fire.

Then prostrate falls, and begs with ardent eyes

Soon to obtain, and long possess the prize:

The powers gave ear, and granted half his prayer;

The rest the winds dispersed in empty air.

But now secure the painted vessel glides,

The sun-beams trembling on the floating tides:

While melting music steals upon the sky,

And soften'd sounds along the water die;

Smooth flow the waves, the zephyrs gently play,

Belinda smiled, and all the world was gay,

All but the Sylph; with careful thoughts oppress'd,

The impending woe sat heavy on his breast:

He summons straight his denizens of air;

The lucid squadrons round the sails repair:
Soft o'er the shrouds aërial whispers breathe,
That seem'd but zephyrs to the train beneath.
Some to the sun their insect wings unfold,
Waft on the breeze, or sink in clouds of gold;
Transparent forms, too fine for mortal sight,
Their fluid bodies half dissolved in light.
Loose to the wind their airy garments flew,
Thin glittering textures of the filmy dew,
Dipp'd in the richest tinctures of the skies,
Where light disports in ever-mingling dyes,
Where every beam new transient colours flings,
Colours that change whene'er they wave their wings.
Amid the circle on the gilded mast,
Superior by the head, was Ariel placed;
His purple pinions opening to the sun,
He raised his azure wand, and thus begun:
  "Ye Sylphs and Sylphids, to your chief give ear;
Fays, Fairies, Genii, Elves, and Demons, hear:
Ye know the spheres, and various tasks assign'd

By laws eternal to the aërial kind.

Some in the fields of purest ether play,

And bask and whiten in the blaze of day;

Some guide the course of wandering orbs on high,

Or roll the planets through the boundless sky;

Some, less refined, beneath the moon's pale light

Pursue the stars that shoot athwart the night,

Or suck the mists in grosser air below,

Or dip their pinions in the painted bow,

Or brew fierce tempests on the wintry main,

Or o'er the glebe distil the kindly rain.

Others on earth, o'er human race preside,

Watch all their ways, and all their actions guide:

Of these the chief the care of nations own,

And guard with arms divine the British throne.

  "Our humbler province is to tend the fair,

Not a less pleasing, though less glorious care;

To save the powder from too rude a gale,

Nor let the imprison'd essences exhale;

To draw fresh colours from the vernal flowers;

To steal from rainbows, ere they drop in showers,
A brighter wash; to curl their waving hairs,
Assist their blushes, and inspire their airs;
Nay, oft in dreams, invention we bestow,
To change a flounce or add a furbelow.

"This day, black omens threat the brightest fair
That e'er deserved a watchful spirit's care:
Some dire disaster, or by force, or slight;
But what, or where, the Fates have wrapp'd in night.
Whether the nymph shall break Diana's law,
Or some frail china jar receive a flaw:
Or stain her honour, or her new brocade;
Forget her prayers, or miss a masquerade;
Or lose her heart, or necklace at a ball;
Or whether Heaven has doom'd that Shock must fall.
Haste then, ye spirits! to your charge repair:
The fluttering fan be Zephyretta's care;
The drops to thee, Brillante, we consign;
And, Momentilla, let the watch be thine;
Do thou, Crispissa, tend her favourite lock;

Ariel himself shall be the guard of Shock.

"To fifty chosen Sylphs, of special note,
We trust the important charge, the petticoat:
Oft have we known that sevenfold fence to fail,   '
Though stiff with hoops, and arm'd with ribs of whale,
Form a strong line about the silver bound,
And guard the wide circumference around.

"Whatever spirit, careless of his charge,
His post neglects, or leaves the fair at large,
Shall feel sharp vengeance soon o'ertake his sins;
Be stopp'd in vials, or transfix'd with pins;
Or plunged in lakes of bitter washes lie,
Or wedged whole ages in a bodkin's eye:
Gums and pomatums shall his flight restrain,
While clogg'd he beats his silken wings in vain;
Or alum styptics, with contracting power,
Shrink his thin essence like a shrivel'd flower:
Or, as Ixion fix'd, the wretch shall feel
The giddy motion of the whirling mill,
In fumes of burning chocolate shall glow,

And tremble at the sea that froths below!"

He spoke; the spirits from the sails descend;
Some, orb in orb, around the nymph extend;
Some thrid the mazy ringlets of her hair;
Some hang upon the pendants of her ear;
With beating hearts the dire event they wait,
Anxious, and trembling for the birth of fate.

CANTO III

CLOSE by those meads, for ever crown'd with flowers,

Where Thames with pride surveys his rising towers,

There stands a structure of majestic frame,

Which from the neighbouring Hampton takes its name.

Here Britain's statesmen oft the fall foredoom

Of foreign tyrants, and of nymphs at home;

Here thou, great Anna! whom three realms obey,

Dost sometimes counsel take — and sometimes tea.

  Hither the heroes and the nymphs resort,

To taste awhile the pleasures of a court;

In various talk the instructive hours they pass'd,

Who gave the ball, or paid the visit last;

One speaks the glory of a British queen,

And one describes a charming Indian screen;

A third interprets motions, looks, and eyes;

At every word a reputation dies.

Snuff, or the fan, supply each pause of chat,

With singing, laughing, ogling, and all that.

Meanwhile, declining from the noon of day,

The sun obliquely shoots his burning ray:

The hungry judges soon the sentence sign,

And wretches hang that jurymen may dine;

The merchant from the Exchange returns in peace,

And the long labours of the toilet cease,

Belinda now, whom thirst of fame invites,

Burns to encounter two adventurous knights,

At Ombre singly to decide their doom;

And swells her breast with conquests yet to come.

Straight the three bands prepare in arms to join,

Each band the number of the sacred nine.

Soon as she spreads her hand, the aërial guard

Descend, and sit on each important card:

First Ariel perch'd upon a Matadore,

Then each according to the rank they bore;

For Sylphs, yet mindful of their ancient race,

Are, as when women, wondrous fond of place.

Behold, four kings in majesty revered,

With hoary whiskers and a forky beard;

And four fair queens, whose hands sustain a flower,

The expressive emblem of their softer power;

Four knaves in garbs succinct, a trusty band;

Caps on their heads, and halberts in their hand;

And party-colour'd troops, a shining train,

Drawn forth to combat on the velvet plain.

The skilful nymph reviews her force with care.

"Let spades be trumps!" she said, and trumps they were.

Now move to war her sable Matadores,

In show like leaders of the swarthy Moors.

Spadillio first, unconquerable lord,

Led off two captive trumps, and swept the board.

As many more Manillio forced to yield,

And march'd a victor from the verdant field.

Him Basto follow'd, but his fate more hard

Gain'd but one trump, and one plebeian card.

With his broad sabre next, a chief in years,

The hoary majesty of Spades appears,

Puts forth one manly leg, to sight reveal'd,

The rest his many-colour'd robe conceal'd.

The rebel knave, who dares his prince engage,

Proves the just victim of his royal rage.

E'en mighty Pam, that kings and queens o'erthrew,

And mow'd down armies in the fights of Loo,

Sad chance of war! now destitute of aid,

Falls undistinguish'd by the victor Spade!

　　Thus far both armies to Belinda yield;

Now to the baron Fate inclines the field.

His warlike Amazon her host invades,

The imperial consort of the crown of Spades.

The Club's black tyrant first her victim died,

Spite of his haughty mien, and barbarous pride:

What boots the regal circle on his head,

His giant limbs in state unwieldy spread;

That long behind he trails his pompous robe,

And, of all monarchs, only grasps the globe?

　　The baron now his Diamonds pours apace;

26

The embroider'd king who shows but half his face,

And his refulgent queen with powers combined,

Of broken troops an easy conquest find.

Clubs, Diamonds, Hearts, in wild disorder seen,

With throngs promiscuous strow the level green.

Thus when dispersed a routed army runs,

Of Asia's troops, and Afric's sable sons,

With like confusion different nations fly,

Of various habit, and of various dye.

The pierced battalions disunited fall,

In heaps on heaps; one fate o'erwhelms them all.

　The knave of Diamonds tries his wily arts,

And wins (oh shameful chance!) the queen of Hearts.

At this, the blood the virgin's cheek forsook,

A livid paleness spreads o'er all her look;

She sees, and trembles at the approaching ill,

Just in the jaws of ruin, and Codille.

And now (as oft in some distemper'd state)

On one nice trick depends the general fate,

An ace of Hearts steps forth: the king unseen

Lurk'd in her hand, and mourn'd his captive queen:

He springs to vengeance with an eager pace,

And falls like thunder on the prostrate ace.

The nymph exulting fills with shouts the sky;

The walls, the woods, and long canals reply.

    O thoughtless mortals! ever blind to fate,

Too soon dejected, and too soon elate.

Sudden, these honours shall be snatch'd away,

And cursed for ever this victorious day.

    For lo! the board with cups and spoons is crown'd,

The berries crackle, and the mill turns round:

On shining altars of Japan they raise

The silver lamp; the fiery spirits blaze:

From silver spouts the grateful liquors glide,

While China's earth receives the smoking tide;

At once they gratify their scent and taste,

And frequent cups prolong the rich repast.

Straight hover round the fair her airy band;

Some, as she sipp'd, the fuming liquor fann'd,

Some o'er her lap their careful plumes display'd,

Trembling, and conscious of the rich brocade.

Coffee (which makes the politician wise,

And see through all things with his half-shut eyes)

Sent up in vapours to the baron's brain

New stratagems, the radiant lock to gain.

Ah cease, rash youth; desist ere't is too late,

Fear the just gods, and think of Scylla's fate!

Changed to a bird, and sent to flit in air,

She dearly paid for Nisus' injured hair!

But when to mischief mortals bend their will,

How soon they find fit instruments of ill!

Just then, Clarissa drew, with tempting grace,

A two-edged weapon from her shining case;

So ladies, in romance, assist their knight,

Present the spear, and arm him for the fight.

He takes the gift with reverence, and extends

The little engine on his fingers' ends;

This just behind Belinda's neck he spread,

As o'er the fragrant steams she bends her head

Swift to the lock a thousand sprites repair,

A thousand wings, by turns, blow black the hair!

And thrice they twitch'd the diamond in her ear;

Thrice she look'd back, and thrice the foe drew near.

Just in that instant, anxious Ariel sought

The close recesses of the virgin's thought;

As on the nosegay in her breast reclined,

He watch'd the ideas rising in her mind,

Sudden he view'd, in spite of all her art,

An earthly lover lurking at her heart.

Amazed, confused, he found his power expired,

Resign'd to fate, and with a sigh retired.

The peer now spreads the glittering forfex wide,

To enclose the lock; now joins it, to divide.

E'en then, before the fatal engine closed,

A wretched Sylph too fondly interposed;

Fate urged the shears, and cut the Sylph in twain

(But airy substance soon unites again),

The meeting points the sacred hair dissever

From the fair head, for ever, and for ever!

The peer now spreads the glittering forfex wide,

Then flash'd the living lightning from her eyes,

And streams of horror rend the affrighted skies.

Not louder shrieks to pitying Heaven are cast,

When husbands, or when lap-dogs, breathe their last!

Or when rich china vessels, fallen from high,

In glittering dust and painted fragments lie!

"Let wreaths of triumph now my temples twine

(The victor cried); the glorious prize is mine!

While fish in streams, or birds delight in air,

Or in a coach and six the British fair;

As long as Atalantis shall be read,

Or the small pillow grace a lady's bed;

While visits shall be paid on solemn days,

When numerous wax-lights in bright order blaze;

While nymphs take treats, or assignations give,

So long my honour, name, and praise shall live!

What time would spare from steel receives its date,

And monuments, like men, submit to fate:

Steel could the labour of the gods destroy,

And strike to dust the imperial towers of Troy;

Steel could the works of mortal pride confound,

And hew triumphal arches to the ground.

What wonder then, fair nymph! thy hairs should feel

The conquering force of unresisted steel?"

CANTO IV

BUT anxious cares the pensive nymph oppress'd,

And secret passions labour'd in her breast.

Not youthful kings in battle seized alive,

Not scornful virgins who their charms survive,

Not ardent lovers robb'd of all their bliss,

Not ancient ladies when refused a kiss,

Not tyrants fierce that unrepenting die,

Not Cynthia when her manteau's pinn'd awry,

E'er felt such rage, resentment, and despair,

As thou, sad virgin! for thy ravish'd hair.

For, that sad moment, when the Sylphs withdrew,

And Ariel weeping from Belinda flew,

Umbriel, a dusky, melancholy sprite,

As ever sullied the fair face of light,

Down to the central earth, his proper scene,

Repair'd to search the gloomy cave of Spleen.

Swift on his sooty pinions flits the Gnome,

And in a vapour reach'd the dismal dome.

No cheerful breeze this sullen region knows,

The dreaded east is all the wind that blows.

Here in a grotto, shelter'd close from air,

And screen'd in shades from day's detested glare,

She sighs for ever on her pensive bed,

Pain at her side, and Megrim at her head.

    Two handmaids wait the throne; alike in place,

But differing far in figure and in face.

Here stood Ill-nature like an ancient maid,

Her wrinkled form in black and white array'd;

With store of prayers, for mornings, nights, and noons,

Her hand is fill'd; her bosom with lampoons.

There Affectation, with a sickly mien,

Shows in her cheek the roses of eighteen,

Practised to lisp, and hang the head aside,

Faints into airs, and languishes with pride,

On the rich quilt sinks with becoming woe,

Wrapp'd in a gown, for sickness, and for show.

The fair ones feel such maladies as these,

When each new night-dress gives a new disease.

A constant vapour o'er the palace flies;

Strange phantoms rising as the mists arise;

Dreadful, as hermits' dreams in haunted shades,

Or bright, as visions of expiring maids.

Now glaring fiends, and snakes on rolling spires,

Pale spectres, gaping tombs, and purple fires:

Now lakes of liquid gold, Elysian scenes,

And crystal domes, and angels in machines.

Unnumber'd throngs on every side are seen,

Of bodies changed to various forms by Spleen.

Here living tea-pots stand, one arm held out,

One bent; the handle this, and that the spout:

A pipkin there, like Homer's tripod walks;

Here sighs a jar, and there a goose-pie talks;

Men prove with child, as powerful fancy works,

And maids, turn'd bottles, call aloud for corks.

Safe pass'd the Gnome through this fantastic band,

A branch of healing spleen-wort in his hand,

Then thus address'd the power: "Hail, wayward queen!

Who rule the sex to fifty from fifteen:

Parent of vapours, and of female wit,

Who give the hysteric, or poetic fit,

On various tempers act by various ways,

Make some take physic, others scribble plays;

Who cause the proud their visits to delay,

And send the godly in a pet to pray.

A nymph there is, that all thy power disdains,

And thousands more in equal mirth maintains.

But, oh! if e'er thy Gnome could spoil a grace,

Or raise a pimple on a beauteous face,

Like citron-waters, matrons' cheeks inflame,

Or change complexions at a losing game;

If e'er with airy horns I planted heads,

Or rumpled petticoats, or tumbled beds,

Or caused suspicion when no soul was rude,

Or discomposed the head-dress of a prude,

Or e'er to costive lap-dogs gave disease,

Which not the tears of brightest eyes could ease:

Hear me, and touch Belinda with chagrin:
That single act gives half the world the spleen."
  The goddess with a discontented air
Seems to reject him, though she grants his prayer.
A wondrous bag with both her hands she binds,
Like that where once Ulysses held the winds;
There she collects the force of female lungs,
Sighs, sobs, and passions, and the war of tongues.
A vial next she fills with fainting fears,
Soft sorrows, melting griefs, and flowing tears.
The Gnome rejoicing bears her gifts away,
Spreads his black wings, and slowly mounts to day.
  Sunk in Thalestris' arms the nymph he found,
Her eyes dejected, and her hair unbound.
Full o'er their heads the swelling bag he rent,
And all the furies issued at the vent.
Belinda burns with more than mortal ire,
And fierce Thalestris fans the rising fire.
"O wretched maid!" she spread her hands, and cried
(While Hampton's echoes, "wretched maid!" replied),

"Was it for this you took such constant care
The bodkin, comb, and essence to prepare?
For this your locks in paper durance bound?
For this with torturing irons wreathed around?
For this with fillets strain'd your tender head,
And bravely bore the double loads of lead?
Gods! shall the ravisher display your hair,
While the fops envy, and the ladies stare?
Honour forbid! at whose unrival'd shrine
Ease, pleasure, virtue, all our sex resign.
Methinks already I your tears survey,
Already hear the horrid things they say,
Already see you a degraded toast,
And all your honour in a whisper lost!
How shall I, then, your hapless fame defend?
'T will then be infamy to seem your friend!
And shall this prize, the inestimable prize,
Exposed through crystal to the gazing eyes,
And heighten'd by the diamond's circling rays,
On that rapacious hand for ever blaze?

Sooner shall grass in Hyde-park circus grow,

And wits take lodgings in the sound of Bow!

Sooner let air, earth, sea, to chaos fall,

Men, monkeys, lap-dogs, parrots, perish all!"

   She said; then raging to Sir Plume repairs,

And bids her beau demand the precious hairs

(Sir Plume, of amber snuff-box justly vain,

And the nice conduct of a clouded cane):

With earnest eyes, and round unthinking face,

He first the snuff-box open'd, then the case,

And thus broke out: — "My Lord, why, what the devil?

Z–ds! damn the lock; 'fore Gad, you must be civil!

Plague on't, 't is past a jest — nay prithee, pox!

Give her the hair," — he spoke, and rapp'd his box.

   "It grieves me much (replied the peer again)

Who speaks so well should ever speak in vain;

But by this lock, this sacred lock, I swear

(Which never more shall join its parted hair;

Which never more its honours shall renew,

Clipp'd from the lovely head where late it grew)

That while my nostrils draw the vital air,

This hand, which won it, shall for ever wear."

He spoke, and speaking, in proud triumph spread

The long-contended honours of her head.

But Umbriel, hateful Gnome! forbears not so;

He breaks the vial whence the sorrows flow.

Then see! the nymph in beauteous grief appears,

Her eyes half-languishing, half-drown'd in tears;

On her heaved bosom hung her drooping head,

Which, with a sigh, she raised; and thus she said:

"For ever cursed be this detested day,

Which snatch'd my best, my favourite curl away.

Happy! ah ten times happy had I been,

If Hampton-Court these eyes had never seen!

Yet am not I the first mistaken maid

By love of courts to numerous ills betray'd.

Oh had I rather unadmired remain'd

In some lone isle, or distant northern land;

Where the gilt chariot never marks the way,

Where none learn ombre, none e'er taste bohea!

There kept my charms conceal'd from mortal eye,

Like roses, that in deserts bloom and die.

What moved my mind 'with youthful lords to roam?

Oh had I staid, and said my prayers at home!

'T was this, the morning omens seem'd to tell;

Thrice from my trembling hand the patch-box fell;

The tottering china shook without a wind,

Nay, Poll sat mute, and Shock was most unkind!

A Sylph too warn'd me of the threats of fate,

In mystic visions, now believed too late!

See the poor remnants of these slighted hairs!

My hand shall rend what e'en thy rapine spares:

These in two sable ringlets taught to break,

Once gave new beauties to the snowy neck;

The sister-lock now sits uncouth, alone,

And in its fellow's fate foresees its own;

Uncurl'd it hangs, the fatal shears demands,

And tempts, once more, thy sacrilegious hands.

Oh hadst thou, cruel! been content to seize

Hairs less in sight, or any hairs but these!"

CANTO V

SHE said; the pitying audience melt in tears;
But Fate and Jove had stopp'd the baron's ears.
In vain Thalestris with reproach assails,
For who can move when fair Belinda fails?
Not half so fix'd the Trojan could remain,
While Anna begg'd, and Dido raged in vain.
Then grave Clarissa graceful waved her fan;
Silence ensued, and thus the nymph began:

"Say, why are beauties praised and honour'd most,
The wise man's passion, and the vain man's toast?
Why deck'd with all that land and sea afford?
Why angels call'd, and angel-like adored?
Why round our coaches crowd the white-gloved beaux?
Why bows the side-box from its inmost rows?
How vain are all these glories, all our pains,

Unless good sense preserve what beauty gains:

That men may say, when we the front-box grace,

Behold the first in virtue as in face!

Oh! if to dance all night and dress all day,

Charm'd the small-pox, or chased old age away,

Who would not scorn what housewife's cares produce,

Or who would learn one earthly thing of use?

To patch, nay ogle, may become a saint;

Nor could it sure be such a sin to paint.

But since, alas; frail beauty must decay;

Curl'd or uncurl'd, since locks will turn to grey;

Since painted, or not painted, all shall fade,

And she who scorns a man must die a maid;

What then remains but well our power to use,

And keep good-humour still, whate'er we lose?

And trust me, dear! good-humour can prevail,

When airs, and flights, and screams, and scolding fail.

Beauties in vain their pretty eyes may roll;

Charms strike the sight, but merit wins the soul."

So spoke the dame, but no applause ensued:

Belinda frown'd, Thalestris call'd her prude.

"To arms, to arms!" the fierce virago cries,

And swift as lightning to the combat flies.

All side in parties, and begin the attack;

Fans clap, silks rustle, and tough whalebones crack;

Heroes' and heroines' shouts confusedly rise,

And base and treble voices strike the skies.

No common weapons in their hands are found;

Like gods they fight, nor dread a mortal wound.

So when bold Homer makes the gods engage,

And heavenly breasts with human passions rage;

'Gainst Pallas, Mars; Latona, Hermes arms;

And all Olympus rings with loud alarms;

Jove's thunder roars, Heaven trembles all around,

Blue Neptune storms, the bellowing deeps resound;

Earth shakes her nodding towers, the ground gives way,

And the pale ghosts start at the flash of day!

Triumphant Umbriel on a sconce's height

Clapp'd his glad wings. and sat to view the fight:

Propp'd on their bodkin-spears, the sprites survey

The growing combat, or assist the fray.

While through the press enraged Thalestris flies,
And scatters death around from both her eyes,
A beau and witling perish'd in the throng,
One died in metaphor, and one in song.
"O cruel nymph! a living death I bear,"
Cried Dapperwit, and sunk beside his chair.
A mournful glance Sir Fopling upwards cast;
"Those eyes are made so killing – "was his last.
Thus on Mæander's flowery margin lies
The expiring swan, and as he sings he dies.

When bold Sir Plume had drawn Clarissa down.
Chloe stepp'd in, and kill'd him with a frown;
She smiled to see the doughty hero slain,
But, at her smile, the beau revived again.

Now Jove suspends his golden scales in air,
Weighs the men's wits against the lady's hair;
The doubtful beam long nods from side to side;
At length the wits mount up, the hairs subside.

See fierce Belinda on the baron flies,

With more than usual lightning in her eyes:

Nor fear'd the chief the unequal fight to try,

Who sought no more than on his foe to die.

But this bold lord, with manly strength endued,

She with one finger and a thumb subdued:

Just where the breath of life his nostrils drew,

A charge, of snuff the wily virgin threw;

The Gnomes direct, to every atom just,

The pungent grains of titillating dust.

Sudden with starting tears each eye o'erflows,

And the high dome re-echoes to his nose.

"Now meet thy fate," incensed Belinda cried,

And drew a deadly bodkin from her side.

(The same, his ancient personage to deck,

Her great-great-grandsire wore about his neck,

In three seal-rings; which after, melted down,

Form'd a vast buckle for his widow's gown:

Her infant grandame's whistle next it grew,

The bells she jingled, and the whistle blew;

Then in a bodkin graced her mother's hairs,

Which long she wore, and now Belinda wears).

"Boast not my fall," he cried, "insulting foe!
Thou by some other shalt be laid as low.
Nor think, to die dejects my lofty mind:
All that I dread is leaving you behind!
Rather than so, ah let me still survive,
And burn in Cupid's flames — but burn alive."

"Restore the lock," she cries; and all around,
"Restore the lock!" the vaulted roofs rebound.
Not fierce Othello in so loud a strain
Roar'd for the handkerchief that caused his pain.
But see how oft ambitious aims are cross'd.
And chiefs contend till all the prize is lost!
The lock, obtain'd with guilt, and kept with pain,
In every place is sought, but sought in vain:
With such a prize no mortal must be bless'd:
So Heaven decrees! with Heaven who can contest?

Some thought it mounted to the lunar sphere,
Since all things lost on earth are treasured there.
There heroes' wits are kept in ponderous vases,

And beaux in snuff-boxes and tweezer-cases;
There broken vows and death-bed alms are found,
And lovers' hearts with ends of riband bound;
The courtiers' promises, and sick-man's prayers,
The smiles of harlots, and the tears of heirs,
Cages for gnats, and chains to yoke a flea,
Dried butterflies, and tomes of casuistry.

But trust the muse — she saw it upward rise,
Though mark'd by none but quick poetic eyes;
(So Rome's great founder to the heavens withdrew,
To Proculus alone confess'd in view):
A sudden star, it shot through liquid air,
And drew behind a radiant trail of hair.
Not Berenice's locks first rose so bright,
The heavens bespangling with dishevell'd light.
The Sylphs behold it kindling as it flies,
And pleased pursue its progress through the skies.

This the beau-monde shall from the Mall survey,
And hail with music its propitious ray.
This the bless'd lover shall for Venus take,

And send up vows from Rosamonda's lake.

This Partridge soon shall view in cloudless skies,

When next he looks through Galileo's eyes;

And hence the egregious wizard shall foredoom

The fate of Louis, and the fall of Rome.

    Then cease, bright nymph! to mourn thy ravish'd hair,

Which adds new glory to the shining sphere!

Not all the tresses that fair head can boast,

Shall draw such envy as the lock you lost.

For, after all the murders of your eye,

When, after millions slain, yourself shall die;

When those fair suns shall set, as set they must,

And all those tresses shall be laid in dust,

This lock, the muse shall consecrate to fame,

And 'midst the stars inscribe Belinda's name.

ALEXANDER POPE

born at London May 21, 1688, died at Twickenham, May 30, 1744.

SON of Roman-Catholic parents this delicate and deformed boy was brought up in private schools. From his earliest youth he showed a real greed for books and a strange propensity for metric, rime and poetic thought. As, later in life, he would lay a particular stress on his 'precocity' always feigned a bad memory for the chronology of his own poems and would ever be polishing his earlier production, it is rather hard to get an exact view of him as *enfant prodige*. His first mature poems *The Pastoral* and *Windsor Forest*, though composed as early as 1704, were not published before 1709 and 1713. His *Essay on Criticism* which conveys to us an image of Pope's time and his literary knowledge rather than of his personality, appeared in 1711. Suddenly in 1712 we behold the poet developing into mastership, when he produced the delicacy of the 18th century, his *Rape of the Lock*. During his growth into full maturity he undertook his translation of Homer and his edition of Shakespeare. While the former justly bestowed upon him the praise of his contemporaries, and made him financially independant, with the latter he earned the no less justified reproach of those who, together with Lewis Theobald, were even then laying the foundations of modern Shakespearology. As Pope had now entered the most witty and caustic clan of spirits in his time, with his friends Swift, Arbuthnot, Gay and Parnell he formed a mighty phalanx to fight out numerous real and pretended literary feuds: he created his heroi-comical Martinus Scriblerus and for the time being gave the conspicuous central place in his satirical epos *The Dunciad* to Theobald. Under the most important influence of a friendship, which since the twenties of the century linked him to Bolingbroke, he indulged in the study of ethical problems and published a series of letters under the title of *Moral Essays* beside his well-known *Essay on Man,* which inspired Voltaire for his *Loi Naturelle.* In the last years of his life he composed utterly personal adaptations of Horace's Satires and a new edition of the Dunciad, here doing the same doubtful honour to the dramatist Colley Cibber as done before to Theobald.

Pope certainly does not range among those poets who by the loftiness of their style stand beyond the confines of Time. In about the same manner with which medieval painters dress up the figures of the "Passio" with their own garments, the poet adorns whatever he encounters with the costly silk and velvet, with the jabots and lacework of the 18th century. Pope's muse and Belinda are twins. 'Man' in Pope's famous essay, Shakespeare, Heloïse, Horace, Statius' and Homer's heroes as well as Sappho might well have appeared at Mrs. Fermor's garden parties without shocking any Lord Petre for their unwonted exterior. But on the other hand no poet is such a true mirror of his time, none in his epoch has with equal minuteness reflected the 'beau', refined, accomplished and dainty. To approach Greek architecture, go and see the Parthenon, to study scholastic philosophy, shut yourself up with St. Thomas, but to get intimate with the artful chisel work of the poetry of Queen Anne's Age you should always begin with and return to Pope.

PRINTED BY
FR. RICHTER
LEIPZIG

ImTheStory.com

Personalized Classic Books in many genre's

Unique gift for kids, partners, friends, colleagues

Customize:

- Character Names
- Upload your own front/back cover images (optional)
- Inscribe a personal message/dedication on the
  inside page (optional)

Customize many titles Including
- Alice in Wonderland
- Romeo and Juliet
- The Wizard of Oz
- A Christmas Carol
- Dracula
- Dr. Jekyll & Mr. Hyde
- And more...

CPSIA information can be obtained
at www.ICGtesting.com
Printed in the USA
BVHW08s1046290718
522941BV00013B/213/P